Everything is Possible with God

Study Guide

RICK WARREN

EVERYTHING IS POSSIBLE WITH GOD

STUDY GUIDE

UNDERSTANDING THE
SIX PHASES OF
FAITH

Six Sessions

Deliverance

Dead End

Difficulty

Delay

Decision

Dream

ZONDERVAN®

ZONDERVAN.com/
AUTHORTRACKER
follow your favorite authors

ZONDERVAN

Everything Is Possible with God Study Guide
Copyright © 2010 by Rick Warren

Requests for information should be addressed to:

Zondervan, *Grand Rapids, Michigan* 49530

ISBN 978-0-310-67149-7

Cover design: Rob Monacelli
Interior design: Tina Henderson

Printed in the United States of America

10 11 12 13 14 /DCI/ 20 19 18 17 16 15 14 13 12 11 10 9 8 7 6 5 4 3 2 1

CONTENTS

A Note from Rick Warren

How's your faith? Is it strong or weak? Is it steady or stretched? Would you like your faith to be stronger? Well, that's what this study is all about. You see, faith is like a muscle. It needs to be exercised and developed.

God uses a predictable pattern and process to build your faith. It's what I call the Six Phases of Faith. Once you understand these six phases, you can cooperate with God in the process of strengthening your faith and building your character.

Our God is a God of miracles. He has a plan and a purpose for your life, and he always keeps his promises. Do you believe that everything is possible with God? Jesus said, *"According to your faith, will it be done to you"* (Matthew 9:29 NIV). I pray this study will strengthen your faith and prepare you for what God is about to do in your life.

Understanding Your Study Guide

Here is a brief explanation of the features of this study guide:

Looking Ahead/Catching Up: You will open each meeting by briefly discussing a question that will help focus everyone's attention on the subject of the lesson.

Key Verse: Each session you will find a key Bible verse for your group to read together. If someone in the group has a different translation, ask them to read it aloud so the group can get a bigger picture of the meaning of the passage.

Video Lesson: There is a video lesson for the group to watch together each week. Fill in the blanks in the session outline as you watch the video, and be sure to refer back to these outlines during your discussion time.

Living on Purpose: Each video segment is complemented by two application questions for group discussion. There is no reason to rush through the answers. Give everyone ample opportunity to share their thoughts. If you don't get through all of the discussion questions, that's okay.

Prayer Direction: At the end of each session you will find suggestions for your group prayer time. Praying together is one of the greatest privileges of small group life. Please don't take it for granted.

Putting It Into Practice: This is where the rubber meets the road. We don't want to be just hearers of the Word. We also need to be doers of the Word (James 1:22). These assignments are application exercises that will help you put into practice the truths you have discussed in the lesson.

A TIP FOR THE HOST

The study guide material is meant to be your servant, not your master. The point is not to race through the sessions; the point is to take time to let God work in your lives. Nor is it necessary to "go around the circle" before you move on to the next question. Give people the freedom to speak, but don't insist on it. Your group will enjoy deeper, more open sharing and discussion if people don't feel pressured to speak up.

HOW GOD BUILDS YOUR FAITH

Looking Ahead

Take a few minutes to introduce yourselves to your group, and to review the Group Guidelines on page 56.

How do you describe faith?

Key Verse

Everything is possible for the person who has faith.

Mark 9:23 TEV

Video Lesson

Watch the session one Video Lesson now and fill in the blanks in the outline on pages 13 – 15. Refer back to the outline during your group discussion.

HOW GOD BUILDS YOUR FAITH LESSON OUTLINE

Everything is possible for the person who has faith.

Mark 9:23 TEV

According to your faith, will it be done to you.

Matthew 9:29 NIV

THE SIX PHASES OF FAITH

PHASE 1: _____

Nothing happens until someone starts dreaming.

- God's dream will always _____ .

If a dream comes from God you cannot do it on your own. You can only do it by faith.

> *God ... is able to do far more than we would dare to ask or even dream of — infinitely beyond our highest prayers, desires, thoughts, or hopes.*
>
> Ephesians 3:20 LB

> *Without faith it is impossible to please God.*
>
> Hebrews 11:6 NIV

- God's dream will never _____ .

PHASE 2: _____

Nothing is going to happen to your dream until you wake up and put it into action.

- You must _____ .

- You must _____ .

Phase 3: _____

> *These things I plan won't happen right away. Slowly, steadily, surely, the time approaches when the vision will be fulfilled. If it seems slow, do not despair, for these things will surely come to pass. Just be patient! They will not be overdue a single day.*
>
> Habakkuk 2:3 LB

God will not fulfill your dream immediately. Why? Because God wants to work on you before he works on the project.

Phase 4: _____

God uses difficulties to work on your faith and character.

> *At present you may be temporarily harassed by all kinds of trials. This is no accident — it happens to prove your faith, which is infinitely more valuable than gold.*
>
> 1 Peter 1:7 PH

Phase 5: _____

> *At that time we were completely overwhelmed, the burden was more than we could bear, in fact, we told ourselves that this was the end. Yet we believe now that we had this sense of impending disaster so that we might learn to trust, not in ourselves, but in God who can raise the dead.*
>
> 2 Corinthians 1:8 – 9 PH

Dead ends are a part of God's plan for your life.

> *He has rescued us … and he will rescue us in the future. We are confident that he will continue to rescue us.*
>
> 2 Corinthians 1:10 GW

> *I'm expecting the Lord to rescue me again, so that once again I will see his goodness to me.*
>
> Psalm 27:13 LB

Phase 6: _____

The best response to a dead end is to expect God to act. What are you expecting God to do in your life?

Living on Purpose

1. Which phase of faith are you currently in? Briefly explain your answer.

2. Of all the people you know personally, who do you believe has the strongest faith in God? Why is their faith so strong?

Prayer Direction

In what area of your life do you need your faith to be strengthened? Share your prayer requests and then pray for each other. Use the "Small Group Prayer and Praise Report" beginning on page 61 to keep track of your requests.

Putting It Into Practice

Here's something to think about between now and your next small group meeting:

- What are you expecting God to do in your life?

- What do you think God might be waiting for you to do?

GOD'S DREAM
FOR YOUR LIFE

Catching Up

Which stage of life are you in right now: Are you looking forward to a dream, are you living your dream, or have you given up on a dream?

Key Verse

My life is worth nothing to me unless I use it for finishing the work assigned me by the Lord Jesus.

Acts 20:27 NLT

Video Lesson

Watch the session two Video Lesson now and fill in the blanks in the outline on pages 19 – 21. Refer back to the outline during your group discussion.

GOD'S DREAM FOR YOUR LIFE LESSON OUTLINE

"For I know the plans I have for you," declares the Lord, "plans to prosper you and not harm you, plans to give you hope and a future."

Jeremiah 29:11 NIV

• God's dream for you is _____ .

• God's dream for you is _____ .

D_____ ALL MY LIFE TO GOD

You've got to be willing to do whatever God wants you to do, even before he tells you to do it.

Offer yourselves as a living sacrifice to God dedicated to his service.... Do not conform yourselves to the standards of this world, but let God transform you.... Then you will be able to know the will of God — what is good and pleasing to him and is perfect.

Romans 12:1 – 2 TEV

Let us strip off anything that slows us down or holds us back ... and let us run with patience the particular race that God has set before us.

Hebrews 12:1 LB

My life is worth nothing to me unless I use it for finishing the work assigned me by the Lord Jesus.

Acts 20:27 NLT

R_____ TIME ALONE WITH GOD

You cannot get God's dream unless you spend time with God.

Pause a moment ... and listen; consider the wonderful things God does.

Job 37:14 TEV

God speaks to people who take time to listen.

E_____ MY ABILITIES

For we are God's handiwork, created in Christ Jesus to devote ourselves to the good deeds for which God has designed us.

Ephesians 2:10 NEB

God has given each of you some special abilities; be sure to use them to help each other.

1 Peter 4:10 LB

We are saved to serve. Use your talents and gifts to help other people.

Your young men shall see visions, your old men shall dream dreams.

Acts 2:17 NKJV

A_____ WITH GODLY DREAMERS

Hang out with people who are trying to discover God's dream for their life. There's no such thing as a neutral friend. They're either pulling you toward God's dream or pulling you away from it.

As iron sharpens iron, so a friend sharpens a friend.

Proverbs 27:17 NLT

Bad company corrupts good character.

1 Corinthians 15:33 NIV

M_____ MY DREAM PUBLIC

Visualize the dream, then verbalize the dream.

- It gets _____ .

- It attracts _____ .

- It releases _____ .

The one who calls you is faithful and he will do it.
1 Thessalonians 5:24 NIV

LIVING ON PURPOSE

1. What do you believe God's dream is for your life?

2. Review the D.R.E.A.M. steps in the lesson outline. Which of these steps do you need to take?

PRAYER DIRECTION

- The dream phase of faith begins with dedicating all of yourself to God. In prayer, fully surrender your life to him. Invite him to be your Lord, and ask him to open your eyes and give you his vision for your life.

- Pray for each other's prayer requests.

PUTTING IT INTO PRACTICE

Rick said, "God speaks to people who take time to listen."

- If you currently practice a daily quiet time, we encourage you for the next seven days to double the amount of time you usually spend in devotions.

- If a quiet time with God is not part of your daily routine, we encourage you for the next seven days to take ten minutes a day to review and pray about the Bible verses in this week's lesson outline.

HOW TO MAKE WISE DECISIONS

CATCHING UP

How would you define wisdom?

Who is the wisest person you know?

KEY VERSE

*If any of you need wisdom, you should ask God,
and it will be given to you.*

James 1:5 CEV

VIDEO LESSON

Watch the session three Video Lesson now and fill in the blanks in the outline on pages 25 – 27. Refer back to the outline during your group discussion.

HOW TO MAKE WISE DECISIONS LESSON OUTLINE

A dream is worthless unless you wake up and get to work on it.

GOD'S PRINCIPLES FOR MAKING WISE DECISIONS

• _____

Before you do anything else, get God's perspective on the issue.

> *If any of you need wisdom, you should ask God, and it will be given to you.*
>
> James 1:5 CEV

> *A man is foolish to trust himself. But those who use God's wisdom are safe.*
>
> Proverbs 28:26 LB

Ask: _____ ?

• _____

There is no contradiction between faith and fact. It's wise to find out all you can before you make a decision.

> *Every prudent man acts out of knowledge.*
>
> Proverbs 13:16 NIV

> *How stupid to decide before knowing the facts!*
>
> Proverbs 18:13 LB

Ask: _____ ?
before I make this decision?

• _____

> *The more good advice you get, the more likely you are to win.*
>
> Proverbs 24:6 TEV

It is wise to learn from experience, but it is wiser to learn from the experience of others.

Get good advice and you will succeed.

Proverbs 20:18 TEV

Ask: _____ ?

• _____

Every decision has a price tag.

It is a trap for a man to dedicate something rashly and only later to consider his vows.

Proverbs 20:25 NIV

Making a quick decision is not as important as making the right decision, and a right decision is an informed decision.

Don't begin until you count the cost. For who would begin construction of a building without first calculating the cost to see if there is enough money to finish it?... Or what king would go to war against another king without first sitting down with his counselors to discuss whether his army of 10,000 could defeat the 20,000 soldiers marching against him?

Luke 14:28 – 31 NLT

Ask: _____ ?

• _____

A sensible man watches for problems ahead and prepares to meet them. The simpleton never looks and suffers the consequences.

Proverbs 27:12 LB

You can't ignore problems because they are not going to ignore you. Prepare for problems but don't try to solve all of them ahead of time.

Ask: _____ ?

• _____

Fear is at the root of all indecision.

If you wait for perfect conditions, you'll never get anything done.

Ecclesiastes 11:4 LB

Perfectionism paralyzes potential. The basic commitments of life must be made under imperfect conditions.

If God is for us, who can be against us?

Romans 8:31 NIV

Ask: _____ ?

Not to decide is to decide. What decision do you need to make?

Living on Purpose

1. What decision are you facing that could be a step of faith?

2. Which of the six questions in the lesson outline is the most pressing for you right now? Explain.

Prayer Direction

- If you are in the decision phase, call on the Lord as your Counselor (Isaiah 9:6). Ask him for wisdom, discernment, and to help you make the right decision.

- Pray for each other's prayer requests.

Putting It Into Practice

What will you do between now and your next group meeting that will move you forward in the decision phase of faith?

DELAYED BY DESIGN

CATCHING UP

What places come to mind when you hear the word "delay"?

KEY VERSE

*Let us never grow tired of doing what's right, for if we do not
faint, we'll reap our harvest at the right time.*

Galatians 6:9 MNT

VIDEO LESSON

Watch the session four Video Lesson now and fill in the
blanks in the outline on pages 31 – 33. Refer back to the
outline during your group discussion.

DELAYED BY DESIGN LESSON OUTLINE

When Pharaoh finally let the people go, God did not lead them along ... the shortest route to the Promised Land. God said, "If the people are faced with a battle, they might change their minds and return to Egypt."

Exodus 13:17 NLT

• God uses delays to _____ us.

• God uses delays to _____ us.

The Lord led you through the wilderness for all those forty years ... testing you to find out how you would respond, and whether or not you would really obey him.

Deuteronomy 8:2 LB

WHEN YOU'RE IN A DELAY ...

• _____

Fear keeps you in the wilderness and prolongs the delay.

I will never leave you. I will never abandon you.

Hebrews 13:5 TEV

• _____

On the way the people lost their patience and spoke against God and Moses. They complained.

Numbers 21:4 – 5 TEV

Rest in the Lord; wait patiently for him to act.... Don't fret and worry — it only leads to harm.

Psalm 37:7 – 8 LB

Resting can be an act of faith. It means you're waiting on God.

• _____

All the Israelites grumbled against Moses ... "If only we had died in Egypt!... We should choose a leader and go back to Egypt."

Numbers 14:2 – 4 NIV

Don't settle for less than God's best for your life. Instead of fainting, you need to be persistent and pray.

Let us never grow tired of doing what's right, for if we do not faint, we'll reap our harvest at the right time.

Galatians 6:9 MNT

Always pray and never lose heart.

Luke 18:1 PH

They that wait upon the LORD shall renew their strength. They shall mount up with wings like eagles; they shall run, and not be weary; they shall walk, and not faint.

Isaiah 40:31 KJV

• _____

They forgot the many times God showed them his love, and they rebelled against the Almighty at the Red Sea. But he saved them, as he promised.... But they soon forgot what he had done, they had no patience for his plan.

Psalm 106:7 – 8, 13 TEV/NAB

Has God done things for you in the past? Of course he has. And you can count on him to do them again.

I will bless the Lord and not forget the glorious things he does for me.

Psalm 103:2 LB

The Lord is not being slow in carrying out his promises ... rather, he is being patient with you.

2 Peter 3:9 NJB

These things I plan won't happen right away. Slowly, steadily, surely, the time approaches when the vision will be fulfilled. If it seems slow, do not despair, for these things will surely come to pass. Just be patient! They will not be overdue a single day!

Habakkuk 2:3 LB

LIVING ON PURPOSE

1. How has God brought you through delays in the past? What lessons did you learn while you were waiting for him?

2. Review the Bible verses in the lesson outline. Which verse is the most meaningful to you at this time in your life? Why?

PRAYER DIRECTION

- If you are in the delay phase of faith, call on the Lord as your Sustainer (Psalm 54:4). Ask him to give you patience and hope, and to hold you up when you grow weary.

- Before you pray for each other's requests, take a few minutes to offer prayers of thanksgiving for God's blessings in your life.

Putting It Into Practice

Remembering the things God has done in the past will build your faith for your current situation. Take ten minutes during a quiet time this week and make a summary list of all the things God has done for you.

HOW TO DEAL WITH DIFFICULTY

CATCHING UP

How would you complete this sentence? Life would be so much easier if . . .

KEY VERSE

We can rejoice, too, when we run into problems and trials, for we know . . . they help us learn to be patient.

Romans 5:3 LB

VIDEO LESSON

Watch the session five Video Lesson now and fill in the blanks in the outline on pages 37 – 39. Refer back to the outline during your group discussion.

How to Deal with Difficulty Lesson Outline

In this world you will have trouble. But take heart! I have overcome the world.

John 16:33 NIV

In everything we do we show that we are God's servants by enduring troubles, hardships, and difficulties with great patience.

2 Corinthians 6:4 GNB

Three Keys to Dealing with Difficulty

1. Determine _____

Ask: What caused this?

I tried to think this problem through but it was too difficult for me until I went into your Temple.

Psalm 73:16 – 17 TEV

Three Common Mistakes

• We listen to _____

The centurion followed the advice of the pilot and the owner of the ship.

Acts 27:11 NIV

• We follow _____

The majority decided that we should sail on.

Acts 27:12 NIV

• We rely on _____

When a gentle south wind began to blow, they thought they had obtained what they wanted.

Acts 27:13 NIV

2. Determine _____

Ask: What does God want me to learn?

We can rejoice, too, when we run into problems and trials, for we know … they help us learn to be patient. And patience develops strength of character in us and helps us trust God more each time.

Romans 5:3 – 4 LB

Every storm is a school.

Every trial is a teacher.

Every experience is an education.

Every difficulty is for your development.

3. Determine _____

Ask: How should I react?

What happens _____ you is not as important as what happens _____ you.

The Wrong Response to Difficulty

• Don't _____

The ship was caught up by the storm and could not head into the wind; so we gave way to it and were driven along.

Acts 27:15 NIV

• Don't _____

They began to throw the cargo overboard.

Acts 27:18 NIV

Paul said to the centurion and the soldiers, "Unless these men stay with the ship, you cannot be saved." So the soldiers cut the ropes that held the lifeboat and let it fall away.

Acts 27:31 – 32 NIV

- Don't _____

We finally gave up all hope of being saved.

Acts 27:20 NIV

The Right Response to Difficulty

- _____

What are you pretending is not a problem?

*A man who refuses to admit his mistakes can never be successful.
But if he confesses and forsakes them, he gets another chance.*

Proverbs 28:13 LB

- _____

The only way to face a storm is head-on.

- _____

Everything was falling apart in the storm except Paul. Why? Because Paul's confidence was in God, not in the ship.

*Therefore keep up your courage, men, for I have faith in God that
it will happen just as he told me.*

Acts 27:25 NIV

You may be going through a storm right now, and your ship may not make it. But *you* will make it. You may have to get to shore on a broken piece of the ship, but you're going to make it because God is with you. Don't give up.

Living on Purpose

1. Rick said, "Every problem has a purpose, and the purpose is to teach you a lesson.... What happens *to* you is not as important as what happens *in* you." What do you think God is trying to teach you through the difficulties you are facing right now, and how does he want you to respond?

2. What outcome do you believe will bring the most glory to God?

Prayer Direction

- If you are in the difficulty phase of faith, call on the Lord as your Shield (Psalm 28:7). Ask him to give you strength and courage, and to protect you from the evil one.

- Pray for anyone in your group who is going through a storm right now.

Putting It Into Practice

Take a few minutes this week to review each step in the outline from Rick's lesson and ask yourself, "How does this step apply to the difficulty I'm facing?"

FROM DEAD END TO DELIVERANCE

CATCHING UP

Does anyone have a praise report about an answer to your group's prayers for them?

Does anything feel impossible in your life right now?

KEY VERSE

What is impossible with men is possible with God.

Luke 18:27 NIV

VIDEO LESSON

Watch the session six Video Lesson now and fill in the blanks in the outline on pages 45 – 47. Refer back to the outline during your group discussion.

FROM DEAD END TO DELIVERANCE LESSON OUTLINE

Faith is the substance of things hoped for, the evidence of things not seen.

Hebrews 11:1 KJV

WHAT TO DO WHILE YOU'RE WAITING FOR GOD'S DELIVERANCE

- _____ what God can do

The situation may be out of your control, but it's not out of God's control.

Abraham believed in God who gives life to the dead and who creates something out of nothing.

Romans 4:17 NCV

When you face things that are out of your control, you need more than a positive mental attitude. You need faith in God.

What is impossible with men is possible with God.

Luke 18:27 NIV

- _____ on what God has said

When hope was dead within him, Abraham went on hoping in faith.... He relied on the word of God.

Romans 4:18 PH

How do you know when hope is dead? You start using the word "never."

While God was testing him, Abraham still trusted in God and his promises, and so he offered up his son Isaac.

Hebrews 11:17 LB

- _____ with faith

> *Without weakening in his faith, he faced the fact that his body was as good as dead ... and that Sarah's womb was also dead. Yet he did not waver through unbelief.*
>
> Romans 4:19 – 20 NIV

Faith is not denying reality. Faith is facing the facts without being discouraged by them.

> *We fix our eyes not on what is seen, but on what is unseen. For what is seen is temporary, but what is unseen is eternal.*
>
> 2 Corinthians 4:18 NIV

> *Let us fix our eyes on Jesus, the author and perfecter of our faith.*
>
> Hebrews 12:2 NIV

- _____ God to deliver me

What are you expecting God to do? God works in your life according to your expectation.

> *According to your faith will it be done to you.*
>
> Matthew 9:29 NIV

> *But Abraham never doubted ... he praised God for this blessing even before it happened. He was completely sure that God was able to do anything he promised.*
>
> Romans 4:20 – 21 LB

The ultimate form of faith is thanking God in advance for what he is going to do. Abraham praised God for the blessing even before it happened.

> *But this happened so we might not rely on ourselves but on God, who raises the dead. He has delivered us.... He will deliver us ... (and) we have set our hope that he will continue to deliver us.*
>
> 2 Corinthians 1:9 – 10 NIV

Three Kinds of Deliverance

- _____ deliverance

- _____ deliverance

- _____

Jesus can take a hopeless end and turn it into an endless hope.

Living on Purpose

1. What life experiences came to mind as you listened to Rick's message? Does anyone have a story to share of a time when God delivered you from a dead end?

2. What is the most meaningful lesson you have learned in this study? What difference will that lesson make in your life?

Prayer Direction

- If you are in the dead end phase of faith, call on the Lord as your Deliverer (Psalm 18:2). Ask him to restore your hope and trust in him, and to make a way where there is no way.

- Before you pray for each other's requests, thank God for the lessons in faith that he has taught you through this study.

Putting It Into Practice

Your story of faith can change someone else's life. Who do you know who needs to hear about the six phases of faith? What phase are they in right now? Make a plan to share with them the faith-building lessons you have learned through this study.

SMALL GROUP RESOURCES

Helps for Hosts

Top Ten Ideas for Helping Your Group Succeed

Congratulations! as the host of your small group, you have responded to the call to help shepherd Jesus' flock. Few other tasks in the family of God surpass the contribution you will be making. As you prepare to facilitate your group, whether it is one session or the entire series, here are a few thoughts to keep in mind.

Remember you are not alone. God knows everything about you, and he knew you would be asked to facilitate your group. Even though you may not feel ready, this is common for all good hosts. God promises, "I will never leave you; I will never abandon you" (Hebrews 13:5 TEV). Whether you are facilitating for one evening, several weeks, or a lifetime, you will be blessed as you serve.

1. **Don't try to do it alone.** Pray right now for God to help you build a healthy team. If you can enlist a cohost to help you shepherd the group, you will find your experience much richer. This is your chance to involve as many people as you can in building a healthy group. All you have to do is ask people to help. You'll be surprised at the response.

2. **Be friendly and be yourself.** God wants to use your unique gifts and temperament. Be sure to greet people at the door with a big smile … this can set the mood for the whole gathering. Remember, they are taking as big a step as you are to show up at your house! Don't try to do things exactly like another host; do them in a way that fits you. Admit when you don't have an answer and apologize when you make a mistake. Your group will love you for it and you'll sleep better at night.

3. **Prepare for your meeting ahead of time.** Review the session and write down your responses to each question. Pay special attention to the Putting It Into Practice exercises that ask group members to do something other than engage in discussion. These exercises will help your group live what the Bible teaches, not just talk about it.

4. **Pray for your group members by name.** Before you begin your session, take a few moments and pray for each member by name. You may want to review the prayer list at least once a week. Ask God to use your time together to touch the heart of every person in your group. Expect God to lead you to whomever he wants you to encourage or challenge in a special way. If you listen, God will surely lead.

5. **When you ask a question, be patient.** Someone will eventually respond. Sometimes people need a moment or two of silence to think about the question. If silence doesn't bother you, it won't bother anyone else. After someone responds, affirm the response with a simple "thanks" or "great answer." Then ask, "How about somebody else?" or "Would someone who hasn't shared like to add anything?" Be sensitive to new people or reluctant members who aren't ready to say, pray, or do anything. If you give them a safe setting, they will blossom over time. If someone in your group is a wallflower who sits silently through every session, consider talking to them privately and encouraging them to participate. Let them know how important they are to you — that they are loved and appreciated, and that the group would value their input. Remember, still water often runs deep.

6. **Provide transitions between questions.** Ask if anyone would like to read the paragraph or Bible passage. Don't call on anyone, but ask for a volunteer, and then be patient until someone begins. Be sure to thank the person who reads aloud.

7. **Break into smaller groups occasionally.** With a greater opportunity to talk in a small circle, people will connect more with the study, apply more quickly what they're learning, and ultimately get more out of their small group experience. A small circle also

encourages a quiet person to participate and tends to minimize the effects of a more vocal or dominant member.

8. **Small circles are also helpful during prayer time.** People who are unaccustomed to praying aloud will feel more comfortable trying it with just two or three others. Also, prayer requests won't take as much time, so circles will have more time to actually pray. When you gather back with the whole group, you can have one person from each circle briefly update everyone on the prayer requests from their subgroups. The other great aspect of subgrouping is that it fosters leadership development. As you ask people in the group to facilitate discussion or to lead a prayer circle, it gives them a small leadership step that can build their confidence.

9. **Rotate facilitators occasionally.** You may be perfectly capable of hosting each time, but you will help others grow in their faith and gifts if you give them opportunities to host the group.

10. **One final challenge (for new or first-time hosts).** Before your first opportunity to lead, look up each of the five passages that follow. Read each one as a devotional exercise to help prepare you with a shepherd's heart. Trust us on this one. If you do this, you will be more than ready for your first meeting.

Matthew 9:36 – 38 (NIV)

[36]When Jesus saw the crowds, he had compassion on them, because they were harassed and helpless, like sheep without a shepherd. [37]Then he said to his disciples, "The harvest is plentiful but the workers are few. [38]Ask the Lord of the harvest, therefore, to send out workers into his harvest field."

John 10:14 – 15 (NIV)

[14]I am the good shepherd; I know my sheep and my sheep know me — [15]just as the Father knows me and I know the Father — and I lay down my life for the sheep.

1 Peter 5:2 – 4 (NIV)

[2]Be shepherds of God's flock that is under your care, serving as overseers — not because you must, but because you are willing, as God wants you to be; [3]not greedy for money, but eager to serve; not lord-

ing it over those entrusted to you, but being examples to the flock. [4]And when the Chief Shepherd appears, you will receive the crown of glory that will never fade away.

Philippians 2:1 – 5 (NIV)

[1]If you have any encouragement from being united with Christ, if any comfort from his love, if any fellowship with the Spirit, if any tenderness and compassion, [2]then make my joy complete by being like-minded, having the same love, being one in spirit and purpose. [3]Do nothing out of selfish ambition or vain conceit, but in humility consider others better than yourselves. [4]Each of you should look not only to your own interests, but also to the interests of others. [5]Your attitude should be the same as that of Jesus Christ.

Hebrews 10:23 – 25 (NIV)

[23]Let us hold unswervingly to the hope we profess, for he who promised is faithful. [24]And let us consider how we may spur one another on toward love and good deeds. [25]Let us not give up meeting together, as some are in the habit of doing, but let us encourage one another — and all the more as you see the Day approaching.

1 Thessalonians 2:7 – 8, 11 – 12 (NIV)

[7]But we were gentle among you, like a mother caring for her little children. [8]We loved you so much that we were delighted to share with you not only the gospel of God but our lives as well, because you had become so dear to us.... [11]For you know that we dealt with each of you as a father deals with his own children, [12]encouraging, comforting and urging you to live lives worthy of God, who calls you into his kingdom and glory.

Frequently Asked Questions

How Long Will This Group Meet?

This study is six sessions long. We encourage your group to add a seventh session for a celebration. In your final session, each group member may decide if he or she desires to continue on for another study. At that time you may also want to do some informal evaluation, discuss your group guidelines, and decide which study you want to do next. We recommend you visit our website at www.saddlebackresources.com for more video-based small group studies.

Who Is the Host?

The host is the person who coordinates and facilitates your group meetings. In addition to a host, we encourage you to select one or more group members to lead your group discussions. Several other responsibilities can be rotated, including refreshments, prayer requests, worship, or keeping up with those who miss a meeting. Shared ownership in the group helps everybody grow.

Where Do We Find New Group Members?

Recruiting new members can be a challenge for groups, especially new groups with just a few people, or existing groups that lose a few people along the way. We encourage you to use the Circles of Life diagram on page 58 of this study guide to brainstorm a list of people from your workplace, church, school, neighborhood, family, and so on. Then pray for the people on each member's list. Allow each member to invite several people from their list. Some groups fear that newcomers will interrupt the intimacy that members have built over time. However, groups that welcome newcomers generally gain strength with the infusion of new blood. Remember, the next person you add just might become a friend for eternity. Logistically, groups find different ways to add members. Some groups remain permanently open, while others choose to open periodically, such as at the beginning or end of a study. If your group becomes too large for easy, face-to-face conversations, you can subgroup, forming a second discussion group in another room.

How do we handle the child care needs in our group?

Child care needs must be handled very carefully. This is a sensitive issue. We suggest you seek creative solutions as a group. One common solution is to have the adults meet in the living room and share the cost of a babysitter (or two) who can be with the kids in another part of the house. Another popular option is to have one home for the kids and a second home (close by) for the adults. If desired, the adults could rotate the responsibility of providing a lesson for the kids. This last option is great with school-age kids and can be a huge blessing to families.

GROUP GUIDELINES

IT'S A GOOD idea for every group to put words to their shared values, expectations, and commitments. Such guidelines will help you avoid unspoken agendas and unmet expectations. We recommend you discuss your guidelines during session one in order to lay the foundation for a healthy group experience. Feel free to modify anything that does not work for your group.

We agree to the following values:

Clear Purpose	To grow healthy spiritual lives by building a healthy small group community
Group Attendance	To give priority to the group meeting (call if I am absent or late)
Safe Environment	To create a safe place where people can be heard and feel loved (no quick answers, snap judgments, or simple fixes)
Be Confidential	To keep anything that is shared strictly confidential and within the group
Conflict Resolution	To avoid gossip and to immediately resolve any concerns by following the principles of Matthew 18:15 – 17
Spiritual Health	To give group members permission to speak into my life and help me live a healthy, balanced spiritual life that is pleasing to God
Limit Our Freedom	To limit our freedom by not serving or consuming alcohol during small group meetings or events so as to avoid causing a weaker brother or sister to stumble (1 Corinthians 8:1 – 13; Romans 14:19 – 21)
Welcome Newcomers	To invite friends who might benefit from this study and warmly welcome newcomers

Building Relationships To get to know the other members of the group and pray for them regularly

Other _____

We have also discussed and agree on the following items:

Child Care _____

Starting Time _____

Ending Time _____

If you haven't already done so, take a few minutes to fill out the Small Group Calendar on page 60.

Circles of Life

Discover Who You Can Connect in Community

USE THIS CHART to help carry out one of the values in the Group Guidelines, to "Welcome Newcomers."

"Follow me and I will make you fishers of men." (Matthew 4:19 NIV)

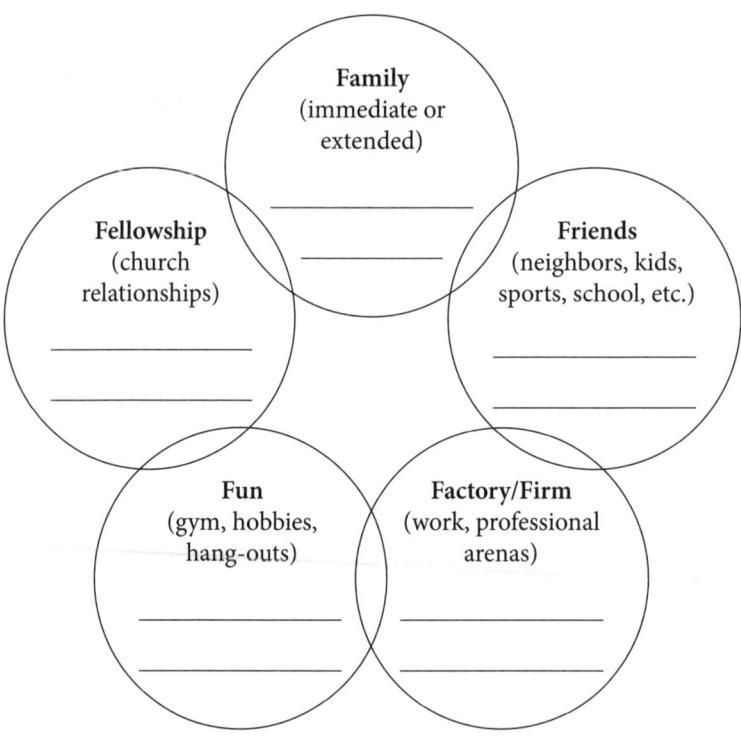

Follow this simple three-step process:

1. List one to two people in each circle.

2. Prayerfully select one person or couple from your list and tell your group about them.

3. Give them a call and invite them to your next meeting. Over 50 percent of those invited to a small group say, "Yes!"

Small Group Calendar

Healthy groups share responsibilities and group ownership. It might take some time for this to develop. Shared ownership ensures that responsibility for the group doesn't fall to one person. Use the calendar to keep track of social events, mission projects, birthdays, or days off. Complete this calendar at your first or second meeting. Planning ahead will increase attendance and shared ownership.

DATE	SESSION	LOCATION	FACILITATOR	SNACK/MEAL
	Session 1			
	Session 2			
	Session 3			
	Session 4			
	Session 5			
	Session 6			
	Celebration			

Small Group Prayer and Praise Report

T HIS IS A place where you can write each other's requests for prayer. You can also make a note when God answers a prayer. Pray for each other's requests. If you're new to group prayer, it's okay to pray silently or to pray by using just one sentence: "God, please help _____ to _____."

DATE	PERSON	PRAYER REQUEST	PRAISE REPORT

DATE	PERSON	PRAYER REQUEST	PRAISE REPORT

DATE	PERSON	PRAYER REQUEST	PRAISE REPORT

DATE	PERSON	PRAYER REQUEST	PRAISE REPORT

Answer Key

Session One: How God Builds Your Faith

Phase 1: <u>Dream</u>
God's dream will always <u>require faith</u>.
God's dream will never <u>contradict God's Word</u>.
Phase 2: <u>Decision</u>
You must <u>invest</u>.
You must <u>let go of security</u>.
Phase 3: <u>Delay</u>
Phase 4: <u>Difficulty</u>
Phase 5: <u>Dead End</u>
Phase 6: <u>Deliverance</u>

Session Two: God's Dream for Your Life

God's dream for you is <u>personal</u>.
God's dream for you is <u>positive</u>.
<u>Dedicate</u> All My Life to God
<u>Reserve</u> Time Alone with God
<u>Evaluate</u> My Abilities
<u>Associate</u> with Godly Dreamers
<u>Make</u> My Dream Public
It gets <u>you started</u>.
It attracts <u>other people's support</u>.
It releases <u>God's power</u>.

SESSION THREE: HOW TO MAKE WISE DECISIONS

Pray for guidance
Ask: What does God want?
Get the facts
Ask: What do I need to know?
Ask for advice
Ask: Who can I talk to?
Calculate the cost
Ask: Is it worth it?
Prepare for problems
Ask: What could go wrong?
Face Your fears
Ask: What am I afraid of?

SESSION FOUR: DELAYED BY DESIGN

God uses delays to prepare us.
God uses delays to test us.
Don't fear
Don't fret
Don't faint
Don't forget

SESSION FIVE: HOW TO DEAL WITH DIFFICULTY

Determine the reason
We listen to bad advice
We follow the crowd
We rely on circumstances
Determine the result
Determine my response
What happens to you is not as important as what happens in you.
Don't drift
Don't discard
Don't despair
Confess my part

Confront it
Claim a promise

SESSION SIX: FROM DEAD END TO DELIVERANCE

Remember what God can do
Rely on what God has said
Face the facts with faith
Expect God to deliver me
Circumstantial deliverance
Personal deliverance
Heaven

Key Verses

ONE OF THE most effective ways to drive deeply into our lives the principles we are learning in this series is to memorize key Scriptures. For many, memorization is a new concept or one that has been difficult in the past. We encourage you to stretch yourself and try to memorize the key verses for this study (below and on page 71). If possible, memorize them as a group and make them part of your group time. You may cut these apart and carry them in your wallet.

I have hidden your word in my heart that I might not
sin against you. (Psalm 119:11 NIV)

Session One

Everything is possible for the person who has faith.

Mark 9:23 TEV

Session Two

My life is worth nothing to me unless I use it for finishing
the work assigned me by the Lord Jesus.

Acts 20:27 NLT

Session Three

If any of you need wisdom, you should ask God,
and it will be given to you.

James 1:5 CEV

SESSION FOUR

Let us never grow tired of doing what's right,
for if we do not faint, we'll reap our harvest at the right time.

Galatians 6:9 MNT

SESSION FIVE

We can rejoice, too, when we run into problems and trials,
for we know ... they help us learn to be patient.

Romans 5:3 LB

SESSION SIX

What is impossible with men is possible with God.

Luke 18:27 NIV

The Purpose Driven® Life
A six-session video-based study for groups or individuals

Embark on a journey of discovery with this video-based study taught by Rick Warren. In it you will discover the answer to life's most fundamental question: "What on earth am I here for?"

And here's a clue to the answer: "It's not about you . . . You were created by God and for God, and until you understand that, life will never make sense. It is only in God that we discover our origin, our identity, our meaning, our purpose, our significance, and our destiny."

Whether you experience this adventure with a small group or on your own, this six-session, video-based study will change your life.

Be sure to combine this study with your reading of the best-selling book, *The Purpose Driven® Life,* to give you or your small group the opportunity to discuss the implications and applications of living the life God created you to live.

Pick up a copy today at your favorite bookstore!

ZONDERVAN®
.com

Better Together

What on Earth Are We Here For?

Rick Warren

The Better Together DVD—part of the Living with Purpose series—is a dynamic individual or small group DVD study from Rick Warren. In each session, you will learn how to fulfill God's five purposes for your life. Each session also includes the biblical support behind each purpose, the ways it applies to you and your circle of influence, and how you can use this knowledge to benefit God's kingdom.

From the beginning, God planned for Christians to fulfill his purposes in community with each other in our church families, small groups, and in the world as a whole. Why did God plan it this way? Because we're better together!

Better Together will deepen your understanding of how God uses community for your own good and growth, as well as help you cultivate deeper relationships with those around you.

Learn to fulfill God's purposes ... discover how we are better together. *Better Together* DVD sessions include:

Session 1: What Matters Most
Session 2: Reaching Out Together
Session 3: Belonging Together
Session 4: Growing Together
Session 5: Serving Together
Session 6: Worshiping Together

This DVD is designed for use with the *Better Together Devotional Journal* and *Better Together Study Guide*.

Available in stores and online!

40 Days of Love
We Were Made for Relationships

Rick Warren

What is your number one priority in life?

Renowned pastor and bestselling author Rick Warren teaches us that LOVE is to be that priority—loving God with all your heart and loving your neighbor as yourself.

But in today's world, consumed with everyday challenges, flooded by distractions, and bombarded with temptations ... how do you arrange your life to make loving God and loving your neighbors your deepest desire, highest aspiration, and constant focus? In this six-session group DVD study with separate study guide, Rick Warren shares practical, Christ-centered advice on how to authentically do just that ... love God and love your neighbor as a normal way of life.

With a focus on the spiritual truths of patience, kindness, truth, and forgiveness, you will learn to love like Jesus—in 40 days.

The six DVD session titles are:

Session One: Love Matters Most
Session Two: Love is Patient, Love is Kind
Session Three: Love Speaks the Truth
Session Four: Love is Forgiving
Session Five: Love is not Selfish
Session Six: The Habits of a Loving Heart

Designed for use with the *40 Days of Love Study Guide*

Available in stores and online!

ZONDERVAN®
.com

God's Answers to Life's Difficult Questions

Rick Warren

Does the Bible really answer some of life's most difficult questions?

How does God provide direction to the common issues that we face?

We live in a world where we all have to deal with the realities of stress, failure, crises, loneliness and change. In this six-session DVD study with separate study guide, renowned pastor and bestselling author Rick Warren takes you inside the Bible to discover answers to six of life's toughest questions. Drawing from the examples of different biblical characters who faced the same issues, Warren offers concise, practical insights you can understand and apply in order to move past everyday struggles and experience a life of purpose, peace and significance.

Life's difficult questions do have answers. Answers from the Bible that can change your outlook – and your life.

The six DVD session titles include:

Session One: How Can I Cope with Stress?
Session Two: How Can I Rebound from Failure?
Session Three: How Can I Be Confident in a Crisis?
Session Four: How Can I Live Above Average?
Session Five: How Can I Overcome Loneliness?
Session Six: How Can I Ever Change?

Say Yes to God

A Call to Courageous Surrender

Kay Warren

You have a plan for the rest of your life. God has a plan for the rest of your life. Are they the same? *Say Yes to God*—formerly titled *Dangerous Surrender*—will help you find the answer.

You have expectations for how your life will play out, and you hope those plans will become realities. But what if God's plan for your life is far different from what you had in mind? Can you accept that? Will you surrender your goals for God's?

Kay Warren had a plan. Together with her husband, Rick Warren, author of the megaseller *The Purpose Driven Life*, she planned that after her kids were grown, she'd travel the world, teaching and encouraging couples in ministry. It was a good plan. But it wasn't what God had in mind for her.

In her own startling wake-up call, Kay discovered the shocking realities of the AIDS pandemic in Africa while reading a magazine. "I want to use you!" she heard God say. That began the struggle—first to avoid God's call and then to surrender herself to God.

If you've ever struggled with knowing and doing God's will, this book is for you. With raw honesty, Kay goes straight to the heart of the matter: the bottom line is surrender. Will you say yes to God? Kay Warren took that step and the decision transformed her life and reshaped her future. She invites you to do the same.

You'll benefit most by discussing this book with others. A Readers' Group Discussion Guide is provided in the back of the book. Additional help can be found at www.kaywarren.com.

Available in stores and online!

Foundations: 11 Core Truths to Build Your Life On

Taught by Tom Holladay and Kay Warren

Foundations is a series of 11 four-week video studies covering the most important, foundational doctrines of the Christian faith. Study topics include:

The Bible—This study focuses on where the Bible came from, why it can be trusted, and how it can change your life.

God—This study focuses not just on facts about God, but on how to know God himself in a more powerful and personal way.

Jesus—As we look at what the Bible says about the person of Christ, we do so as people who are developing a lifelong relationship with Jesus.

The Holy Spirit—This study focuses on the person, the presence, and the power of the Holy Spirit, and how you can be filled with the Holy Spirit on a daily basis.

Creation—Each of us was personally created by a loving God. This study does not shy away from the great scientific and theological arguments that surround the creation/evolution debate. However, you will find the goal of this study is deepening your awareness of God as your Creator.